Outgoing

ORIENTAL
SHORTHAIRS

CURIOUS! ACTIVE! SLENDER!

ELEGANT! SMART! VOCAL!

ABDO
Publishing Company

Katherine Hengel

Consulting Editor, Diane Craig, M.A./Reading Specialist

visit us at www.abdopublishing.com

Published by ABDO Publishing Company, a division of ABDO, P.O. Box 398166, Minneapolis, Minnesota 55439. Copyright © 2012 by Abdo Consulting Group, Inc. International copyrights reserved in all countries. No part of this book may be reproduced in any form without written permission from the publisher. Super SandCastle™ is a trademark and logo of ABDO Publishing Company.

Printed in the United States of America, North Mankato, Minnesota
062011
092011

♻ PRINTED ON RECYCLED PAPER

Editor: Liz Salzmann
Content Developer: Nancy Tuminelly
Cover and Interior Design and Production:
   Anders Hanson, Mighty Media
Illustrations: Bob Doucet
Photo Credits: Shutterstock

Library of Congress Cataloging-in-Publication Data
Hengel, Katherine.
 Outgoing Oriental shorthairs / authored by Katherine Hengel ; illustrated by Bob Doucet.
    p. cm. -- (Cat craze. Set 2)
  ISBN 978-1-61714-831-6
 1. Oriental shorthair cat--Juvenile literature. I. Doucet, Bob, ill. II. Title.
  SF449.O73H46 2012
  636.8'2--dc22
                         2010053270

Super SandCastle™ books are created by a team of professional educators, reading specialists, and content developers around five essential components—phonemic awareness, phonics, vocabulary, text comprehension, and fluency—to assist young readers as they develop reading skills and strategies and increase their general knowledge. All books are written, reviewed, and leveled for guided reading, early reading intervention, and Accelerated Reader® programs for use in shared, guided, and independent reading and writing activities to support a balanced approach to literacy instruction.

CONTENTS

The
ORIENTAL SHORTHAIR

Oriental shorthairs love to play. They are thin and strong. They are curious cats that like to share their feelings. They meow and purr a lot!

FACIAL FEATURES

Head

Oriental shorthairs have large heads.

Muzzle

Their **muzzles** are long and thin.

Eyes

Oriental shorthairs often have blue or green eyes.

Ears

Their ears are large! They are very wide at the base.

BODY BASICS

Size

Adult Oriental shorthairs weigh about 7 to 9 pounds (3 to 4 kg).

Build

They have long, thin bodies. Their **muscles** are firm.

Tail

Oriental shorthairs have long, pointy tails.

Legs and Feet

They have long, thin legs. Their paws are small and round.

COAT & COLOR

Oriental Shorthair Fur

Oriental shorthairs don't have a lot of fur. Their coats are short and close to their skin. Their fur is glossy and soft.

Oriental shorthairs come in more than 300 colors! Their coats can be all one color. Or they can be many colors! Some have several colors on a single strand of hair! This is called ticked fur.

ORANGE SPOTTED FUR

ORANGE SPOTTED

Oriental shorthairs come in many different colors and patterns. The photos on these pages show just a few examples.

BROWN SPOTTED FUR

BLACK SMOKE FUR

BROWN TICKED FUR

BROWN SPOTTED

BLACK SMOKE

BROWN TICKED

HEALTH & CARE

Life Span

Oriental shorthairs can live for more than 15 years!

Health Concerns

Some Oriental shorthairs have heart problems. But most are very healthy. They act like kittens their whole lives!

VET'S CHECKLIST

- Have your Oriental shorthair spayed or neutered. This will prevent unwanted kittens.

- Visit a vet for regular checkups.

- Ask your vet which types of food and litter are right for your Oriental shorthair.

- Clean your Oriental shorthair's teeth and ears once a week.

- Ask your vet about shots that may benefit your cat.

ATTITUDE & BEHAVIOR

Personality

Oriental shorthairs are **social**. They love attention! They are curious and smart. They like to explore. They are also very good around children and other pets.

Activity Level

Oriental shorthairs are active. They love to play! Many even fetch. They can make a toy out of anything. They will even help you tie your shoes and read books!

All About Me

Hi! My name is Olive. I'm an Oriental shorthair. I just wanted to let you know a few things about me. I made some lists below of things I like and dislike. Check them out!

Things I Like

- Playing with toys
- Exploring the refrigerator
- Hanging out with other animals
- Playing fetch
- Following my owner around
- Meowing loudly for attention

Things I Dislike

- Being alone for a long time
- Not having any toys
- Not getting enough attention
- Getting bored
- Not having any friends

LITTERS & KITTENS

Litter Size

Females usually give birth to five to seven kittens.

Diet

Newborn kittens drink their mother's milk. They can begin to eat kitten food when they are about six weeks old. Kitten food is different from cat food. It has the extra **protein**, fat, **vitamins**, and **minerals** that kittens need to grow.

Growth

Oriental shorthair kittens should stay with their mother until they are two to three months old. An Oriental shorthair will be almost full grown when it is six months old. But it will continue to grow slowly until it is one year old.

BUYING AN ORIENTAL SHORTHAIR

Choosing a Breeder

It's best to buy a kitten from a **breeder**, not a pet store. When you visit a cat breeder, ask to see the mother and father of the kittens. Make sure the parents are healthy, friendly, and well behaved.

Picking a Kitten

Choose a kitten that isn't too active or too shy. If you sit down, some of the kittens may come over to you. One of them might be the right one for you!

Is It the Right Cat for You?

Buying a cat is a big decision. You'll want to make sure your new pet suits your lifestyle.

Get out a piece of paper. Draw a line down the middle.

Read the statements listed here. Each time you agree with a statement from the left column, make a mark on the left side of your paper. When you agree with a statement from the right column, make a mark on the right side of your paper.

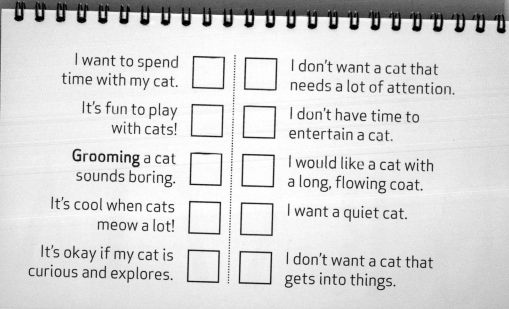

I want to spend time with my cat. ☐   ☐ I don't want a cat that needs a lot of attention.

It's fun to play with cats! ☐   ☐ I don't have time to entertain a cat.

Grooming a cat sounds boring. ☐   ☐ I would like a cat with a long, flowing coat.

It's cool when cats meow a lot! ☐   ☐ I want a quiet cat.

It's okay if my cat is curious and explores. ☐   ☐ I don't want a cat that gets into things.

If you made more marks on the left side than on the right side, an Oriental shorthair may be the right cat for you! If you made more marks on the right side of your paper, you might want to consider another **breed**.

Some Things You'll Need

Cats go to the bathroom in a **litter box**. It should be kept in a quiet place. Most cats learn to use their litter box all by themselves. You just have to show them where it is! The dirty **litter** should be scooped out every day. The litter should be changed completely every week.

Your cat's **food and water dishes** should be wide and shallow. This helps your cat keep its whiskers clean. The dishes should be in a different area than the litter box. Cats do not like to eat and go to the bathroom in the same area.

Cats love to scratch! **Scratching posts** help keep cats from scratching the furniture. The scratching post should be taller than your cat. It should have a wide, heavy base so it won't tip over.

Cats are natural predators. Without small animals to hunt, cats may become bored and unhappy. **Cat toys** can satisfy your cat's need to chase and capture. They will help keep your cat entertained and happy.

Cats should not play with balls of yarn or string. If they accidentally eat the yarn, they could get sick.

Cat claws should be trimmed regularly with special cat claw **clippers**. Regular nail clippers will also work. Some people choose to have their cat's claws removed by a vet. But most vets and animal rights groups think declawing is cruel.

You should brush your cat regularly with a **cat hair brush**. This will help keep its coat healthy and clean.

A **cat bed** will give your cat a safe, comfortable place to sleep.

LIVING WITH AN ORIENTAL SHORTHAIR

Being a Good Companion

Oriental shorthairs need attention. Spend time playing with them each day. They don't need much **grooming**! Just brush them once a week with a cat brush.

Inside or Outside?

It's a good idea to keep your Oriental shorthair inside. Most vets and **breeders** agree that it is best for cats to be kept inside. That way the cats are safe from predators and cars.

Feeding Your Oriental Shorthair

Oriental shorthairs may be fed regular cat food. Your vet can help you choose the best food for your cat.

Cleaning the Litter Box

Like all cats, Oriental shorthairs like to be clean. They don't like smelly or dirty litter boxes. If the litter box is dirty, they may go to the bathroom somewhere else. Ask your vet for advice if your cat isn't using its box.

☠ DANGER: POISONOUS FOODS

Some people like to feed their cats table scraps. Here are some human foods that can make cats sick.

TOMATOES	POTATOES
ONIONS	GARLIC
CHOCOLATE	GRAPES

AN ANCIENT OR A MODERN CAT?

Oriental shorthairs didn't become an official **breed** until the 1950s. But they have been around for centuries! They are related to ancient cats from Siam. Siam is now called Thailand.

We can see cats that look like Oriental shorthairs in a very old book. It's called *The Cat-Book Poems*. It was written between 1350 and 1767! It contains poems and paintings of 17 cats. Some of the cats look just like Oriental shorthairs!

FIND THE ORIENTAL SHORTHAIR

A

B

C

D

THE ORIENTAL SHORTHAIR QUIZ

1. Oriental shorthairs are thin and strong. **True or false?**

2. The Oriental shorthair has a short, wide **muzzle**. **True or false?**

3. Oriental shorthairs have very long coats. **True or false?**

4. Oriental shorthairs can live for more than 15 years. **True or false?**

5. The Oriental shorthair is very curious and smart. **True or false?**

6. Oriental shorthairs are related to cats from South America. **True or false?**

GLOSSARY

breed – a group of animals or plants with common ancestors. A *breeder* is someone whose job is to breed certain animals or plants.

groom – to clean the fur of an animal.

mineral – a natural element that plants, animals, and people need to be healthy.

muscle – the tissue connected to the bones that allows body parts to move.

muzzle – the nose and jaws of an animal.

protein – a substance found in all plant and animal cells.

social – enjoying the company of others.

vitamin – a substance needed for good health, found naturally in plants and meats.